This notebook belongs to:

_____

_____

_____

'Nothing will work unless you do.'
MAYA ANGELOU

'The question isn't who is going to let me; it's who is going to stop me.'

AYN RAND

'If things are not failing, you are not innovating enough.'
ELON MUSK

'I alone cannot change the world, but I can cast a stone across the waters to create many ripples.'

MOTHER TERESA

'I am not afraid. I was born to do this.'

JOAN OF ARC

Disrupter

Disrupter Mantra:
Take the Plunge

Disrupters tend to be *direct* and *resilient* – *unafraid* of making the *bold decisions* that others won't. Disrupters have a *strong vision* for the future and will stop at nothing to get there.

Personality Profile

*Daring * Driven * Provocative*
*Charismatic * Intense*

Disrupters, as their name suggests, are the boldest of the personality types. Purpose-driven and determined to change the world, they work with single-mindedness to transform whatever they turn their attention to – whether that's developing a product, creating a new business model or even shaping a whole industry. Disrupters have an unquenchable thirst for learning and, unlike other personality types, seamlessly convert theoretical knowledge into practice, applying it in the real world. Disrupters are able to to master challenging subjects, come up with solutions quickly and change the way things are done. Playing it safe is not an option for them.

In a work context, Disrupters are self-driven and used to working alone. They can also be inspiring leaders with an infectious vision. A Disrupter is focused and unstoppable until the task is done – working until 3 am doesn't faze a Disrupter – and they may expect others to follow suit. Disrupters are risk-takers, particularly when it comes to their work: pushing beyond their comfort zone is part and parcel of a Disrupter's way of life. If a risk doesn't pay off, they are not afraid to try again until they succeed.

Disrupters are honest and direct, sometimes to the surprise of others. They say things as they are and don't tend to sugarcoat their point or conform to the same social codes as others. At a party, a Disrupter is likely to be the person to bring up a controversial debate or play devil's advocate for the sake of an intellectually stimulating conversation.

Overall, Disrupters lead independent lives. They have a small circle of friends and prefer long-term friendships. Disrupters' friends typically find them hard to read, except the ones they've known since childhood, as Disrupters prefer to guard their feelings and keep their emotions in check. This gives them an air of mystery.

The Big Five Personality Traits

The 'Big Five' model was developed by psychologists in the field of personality science as a framework to describe human personality. The can have five broad traits outlined are: openness to experience, conscientiousness, extraversion, agreeableness and neuroticism – or 'OCEAN' for short.

Disrupters tend to score higher in the personality trait of **OPENNESS TO EXPERIENCE** compared to other personality types. Personality researchers have found that people who are the most open to experience see the world differently: they are more curious, expansive in their thinking, creative and imaginative. Openness reflects a tendency for individuals to be 'cognitive explorers' – deep thinkers who interrogate their own perceptions and emotions, and who are curious and investigative about ideas and philosophical arguments. Disrupters are intellectually enquiring and prefer an innovative approach to something tried and tested. They don't like to stick to the status quo. At the same time, Disrupters are not as free-flowing as other personality types. With clear focus and vision, a Disrupter actively builds towards specific, tangible goals but this can cause tunnel vision, making a Disrupter less open to other ideas and concepts. When they are working on something, they gain comfort from the predictability of their chosen environment.

CONSCIENTIOUSNESS refers to a tendency to be responsible, organised and hard-working. Those who are most conscientious exhibit more goal-oriented behaviour, meaning that, when they make a plan or set a long-term goal, they usually stick to it. They also model good self-regulation and impulse control – for example, if they have an important task to finish, they are usually better at avoiding distraction and procrastination.

Disrupters fall in the middle of the spectrum for conscientiousness. Disrupters craft a long-term vision and work with drive and ambition to get there. But when they're in the zone, a Disrupter is less likely to keep a tidy house and will spend less time and energy on planning and self-discipline, focusing instead on their goals.

EXTRAVERSION refers to an individual's social energy and the conditions they need to recharge. In general, extraverts gain energy through interactions with people, while introverts have less social energy and recharge by spending time alone. It's important to remember that introversion is not to be confused with shyness – introverts can be as sociable and people-loving as extraverts, they just need less stimulation and prefer smaller groups.

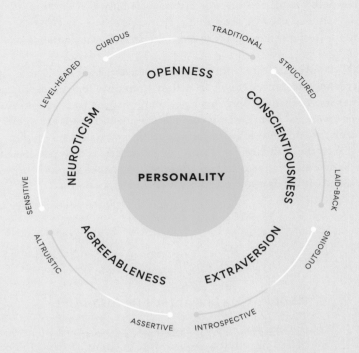

Introvert Disrupters are typically high achievers; they are self-disciplined and good at focusing on the task at hand. They might have a smaller social network but once they develop relationships – intelligently forming close and meaningful bonds – they can have as much influence as extravert Disrupters.

Extravert Disrupters are highly charismatic and persuasive – an asset when it comes to work. They are natural leaders and able to make connections quickly, inspire their team and grow their audience. Extravert Disrupters' social and outgoing tendencies can help them in an entrepreneurial lifestyle, especially when it comes to networking. Their lifestyle is often an unpredictable and chaotic one but extravert Disrupters find their own way to thrive.

AGREEABLENESS refers to an individual's preference for altruism and social harmony. Highly agreeable individuals are less 'me' and more 'we' and they may have a hard time saying no to others or going against the grain. Perceived to be friendly, optimistic and affectionate, people high in agreeableness tend to be empathetic, concerned for the welfare of others and more likely to help those in need. Disrupters tend to score lower on the spectrum of agreeableness than other personality types. They are not afraid to challenge others, find it easier to say no and will comfortably move into the spotlight if a situation demands it.

NEUROTICISM is associated with sensitivity to emotions, self-criticism and general anxiety. Those who score highly in neuroticism tend to experience negative emotions more strongly than other personality types and, therefore, can be less even-tempered. High levels of neuroticism can also result in a more cynical outlook on life and being less comfortable in one's own skin. Disrupters can fall anywhere on the spectrum of neuroticism; however, as they are often highly driven and achievement-oriented, there may be times when Disrupters are preoccupied with their goals to a point bordering on obsession.

5 Books on a Disrupter's Reading List

*Start with Why: How Great Leaders
Inspire Everyone to Take Action*
Simon Sinek

Outliers: The Story of Success
Malcom Gladwell

*In the Company of Women: Inspiration and Advice
from over 100 Makers, Artists, and Entrepreneurs*
Grace Bonney

*The Lean Startup: How Constant Innovation
Creates Radically Successful Businesses*
Eric Ries

Steve Jobs
Walter Isaacson

'I'm convinced that about half of what separates successful entrepreneurs from the non-successful ones is pure perseverance.'

*

STEVE JOBS

Super Powers

VISIONARY THINKING

Disrupters are visionaries: they have a clear picture of the future and a plan for how get there. They can draw order out of chaos and tend to be competent to the point of outperforming others. This skillset makes Disrupters essential for startups and growing businesses – no matter how far-fetched an idea may seem, Disrupters have a unique ability to focus on what is possible and create a plan to achieve it. When Disrupters have a vision in mind, they find ways to inspire and draw people into their vision.

PERSEVERANCE

Disrupters are known for their relentless perseverance. When a Disrupter has a clear vision in mind, they will display great single-mindedness, drive and willpower to achieve it. Few things will deter them and, if they experience setbacks, Disrupters will find new approaches to overcome them. Their resilience is unwavering in the face of failure and this thick-skinned nature can make Disrupters a powerful force.

INNOVATION

Disrupters don't like sticking with the status quo: they value change and finding new, more effective ways of doing things. They criticise those who stay in their comfort zone for the sake of it, because being bold and ambitious is second nature to them. Disrupters are talented at innovation and promoting out-of-the-box ideas that challenge convention.

RESOURCEFULNESS

Disrupters are highly resourceful. They will hustle and find workarounds in the face of unexpected roadblocks and shortages of time, skills and money. Disrupters can often be enterprising and find ways of bending the rules. For a Disrupter, there is nothing worse than settling for mediocrity.

TAKING ACTION

Disrupters are impatient to get things done and can seem to work at double speed. This innate desire for progress, combined with perseverance and resourcefulness makes a Disrupter a powerhouse. Disrupters quickly grasp processes and systems and never settle for complacency – failing is not an option.

Growth Areas

RELIABILITY

As Disrupters are self-driven, they pay less attention to information that doesn't concern them and will often change plans at the last minute if something pressing crops up. This can make them less reliable. Disrupters may be consumed by their own areas of focus and pay less attention to others. They may lose track of time or turn up late to dinners. As a Disrupter, if you find yourself forgetting important dates, keep an up-to-date calendar or set reminders to nudge you.

HEALTHY COMPETITION

Disrupters are often competitive and are not afraid to lose friends if it means winning something. Even when it comes to a friendly game of Monopoly or poker, Disrupters really care about being the victor. When a Disrupter loses, they may take it with less humility than others as they initially feel a hit to their ego. After a loss, a Disrupter will quickly learn what they did wrong and change tactic to ensure they succeed the next time. While competitiveness can be healthy, as a Disrupter be sure to give yourself a break from being constantly 'on' and release your competitiveness harmlessly with friends from time to time.

TACT

Disrupters are not afraid to be direct and honest when a situation or a role demands it. Need an frank opinion on an outfit? You can count on a Disrupter to provide that. Disrupters are strong-willed and, in most situations, believe they are right. At a party, Disrupters are often quicker to judge than others and will be the first to leave a group if they find themselves bored. Extravert Disrupters don't believe in self-censoring, even if this comes at the expense of offending others. While honesty is a virtue, as a Disrupter there may be occasions where you may want to rein it in: check the receptivity of those around you before expressing a controversial opinion.

LETTING GO (A LITTLE)

Disrupters struggle with authority figures. Given their self-belief and drive, they dislike following the lead of others unless they are inspired by them and share the same ideals and goals. This can make Disrupters judgemental and somewhat dismissive. When it comes to mentoring others, they can be impatient, often preferring to do the task themselves if they think they know best. As a Disrupter, try to do a quick assessment of a situation before you take control – you may find there are times when you don't need to take the lead.

RESPOND DON'T REACT

While a Disrupter's unconventional approach can result in innovation and creativity, it can also rub people up the wrong way. Disrupters like to challenge and, at times, provoke by taking a contrarian position. This can be more maladaptive than constructive. Research overwhelmingly indicates that there is a right way to be angry and that channelling anger constructively can help to reduce stress and increase optimism. As a Disrupter, if you feel yourself getting angry, ask yourself which elements of the situation are in your control and what you can do to fix the problem, rather than simply reacting.

Life Hacks

TAKE A BREAK

It is common for Disrupters to be workaholics. They will throw themselves into their work with a drive and focus that can mean that they forget to take breaks in the day, let alone a holiday. As a Disrupter, allow yourself to decompress in order to nurture your own creativity and well-being. For example, take a trip, even if it's just for a day. Whether getting out into nature or going on a roadtrip, a break will do you good.

MANAGE ENERGY, NOT TIME

Disrupters should remember that their energy is what limits what they can do. Instead of focusing on time, Disrupters should consider managing their energy reserves carefully. Think about your patterns of productivity in a typical day – are you most energetic early in the morning or are you a night owl with your greatest focus arriving at night? Work your schedule around your energy levels.

ASK FOR HELP

Disrupters are self-driven and therefore often prefer to do everything themselves. While this is an important part of who they are, Disrupters shouldn't be afraid to ask for help from time to time. Whether it be crowdsourcing a new idea or bouncing a concept around with someone, you can benefit from other people's brain power.

KEEP YOUR WORKSPACE CLEAR

It is important to have a workspace that helps you work. A disorganised desk or a loud space where you are interrupted regularly will detract from your ability to be productive. While you like to mix up your work environment, try to keep wherever you work organised.

EXPAND YOUR MIND

For every personality type, it's important to find a pursuit that calms your mind. As a Disrupter, learning is a means of reducing your stress levels. Take time out every week to read, watch a TED talk or listen to a new podcast.

Compatibility

WHO DO YOU CONNECT WITH?

As Disrupters value achievement and learning, they tend to connect most with those for whom they have a deep respect. A Disrupter has a clear idea of how they want to spend their time: they connect with those from whom they think they can learn and who have a contagious purpose or charisma. Instead of a large group of friends, Disrupters have a few well-chosen close pals with whom they meet regularly. As Disrupters tend to be entrepreneurs who work alone, they rarely mix with colleagues and prefer to keep their work and personal lives separate.

WHO DO YOU CLASH WITH?

As Disrupters value control and need to create their own environment, they are often at odds with those who exert power or authority over them. A Disrupter finds it challenging to work with someone who delegates frequently and who is equally driven by a need for control. Given that they need to maximise time and be productive, Disrupters struggle with those they deem boring or who don't provide them with mental simulation. Disrupters are irked by wasting time and idle chatter, and may call it out when they are uninterested in a conversation. This can be disconcerting to some, who may interpret Disrupters' blunt and direct nature as rudeness. Disrupters won't win a popularity contest but this rarely fazes them.

WHO DO YOU WORK WELL WITH?

Of all the personality types, Disrupters often think they do their best work alone. However, that's not to say that Disrupters don't work well with others. Disrupters are idea generators and connect with similar braniacs. While there's the risk of ego clashes, Disrupters work best with people they respect and admire. Although Disrupters may not be consciously aware of it, they can benefit from a work partner who provides healthy competition, complements their skills and is a good sounding board for new ideas. They will also work well with a partner who is more nurturing and caring and can help prevent them burning out. After a long, tiring day, a supportive teammate can listen and provide much-needed comfort.

WHO DO YOU HAVE A SECRET CRUSH ON?

As curious, knowledgeable individuals, Disrupters like to be challenged intellectually by their romantic partners. They don't have a specific romantic type or need someone to share the same values or interests, but Disrupters will place a premium on intelligence and independence. Disrupters don't like spending too much of their energy on dating or dating apps, so are more likely to rely on serendipity to meet someone or end up turning a close friendship into a relationship.

WHO DO YOU WISH YOU WERE MORE LIKE?

As Disrupters are driven and strongly oriented towards being self-made, they are particularly inspired by individuals who have persevered against all odds and in difficult circumstances. Disrupters are also drawn towards the success stories of those who spearheaded a new way of thinking, creating something out of the ordinary that went against convention. Entrepreneurs who have surmounted personal and professional challenges are likely role models.

In work roles and social situations, introvert Disrupters may aspire to be more like extravert Disrupters, who are comfortable asserting themselves in a large group setting and persuasively bring people into their vision with ease.

5 Famous Disrupters

Michelle Obama * Bill Gates * Steve Jobs

Mark Zuckerberg * Kalpana Chawla

'A vision is
something you
see and others don't.
Some people would
say that's a pocket
definition of lunacy.
But it also defines
entrepreneurial spirit.'

*

ANITA RODDICK

In Friendships and Family

DISRUPTERS VALUE INDEPENDENCE

Disrupters are the most independent of the personality types. They value their time alone and prefer not to make too many commitments or take on obligations that involve others. Disrupters like to structure their time according to their own schedule and make their own decisions, preferring not to compromise on this unless absolutely necessary. Their familial style reflects that: Disrupter parents encourage children to be independent and take responsibility for themselves from a young age.

DISRUPTERS ARE PRAGMATIC

Disrupters are rational and better at addressing problems than emotions. They are inclined to take action and problem solve rather than consider emotional nuances. In a family, they will often leave the emotional conversations to others, preferring to look for a solution over having open, meaningful discussions and offering comfort. This is not to say that Disrupters are not privately sensitive – they just take an overall more pragmatic approach to problems.

DISRUPTERS LIKE MEANINGFUL CONVERSATIONS

Disrupters are keen on maximising time and resources and less so about engaging in gossip and frivolity. When it comes to a catch-up with friends or family, they like to get straight to it, rather than engaging in idle chatter. At a party, you will find a Disrupter sitting outside having a lengthy conversation with a friend rather than joining in the small talk or banter in the kitchen.

DISRUPTERS PREFER LONG-TERM FRIENDSHIPS

Although Disrupters can be sociable in a large group if a situation demands it, they prefer to spend time with their close friends. As Disrupters tend to be more private and direct than other personality types, it's often only their close friends who can get to know their real nature and help a Disrupter stay balanced. They may not meet regularly but they know that they will be there for each other when they are needed.

DISRUPTERS ARE HARD TO READ

Even to their closest friends, Disrupters still have an air of mystery about them. Disrupters like to lead private lives and, while they can be sociable, they generally prefer to keep their feelings to themselves. Disrupters may be animated when talking about their work but less likely to divulge a personal experience or revelation. A Disrupter's friends may have to push them to open up.

In Romantic Relationships

DISRUPTERS ARE NOT DATERS

Disrupters are happy in relationships but get exhausted with the process of starting one, finding the back-and-forth messaging on dating apps a drain on their energy and a waste of time. In a Disrupter's ideal world, they would meet someone incidentally and jump into a relationship as soon as they felt a connection.

DISRUPTERS ARE DIRECT

Both at work and in relationships, a Disrupter won't shy away from conflict and can be more direct and blunt than other personality types, as they are motivated to achieve a resolution. This might not always go down well with a romantic partner. As a Disrupter, take time to explain your communication tendencies to a new romantic partner to spare them a rude awakening.

DISRUPTERS LOVE EXCITEMENT

Disrupters thrive on risk and excitement in both their work and personal lives. They are, therefore, drawn to romantic partners who can also bring some of that energy and excitement to shared activities, whether that's off-the-beaten-track holidays or hobbies at the weekend.

5 Things a Disrupter Will Say

'Anything is possible'

'Try, try and try again'

'You've got to be in it to win it'

'I can always improve'

'Remember why you started'

DISRUPTERS NEED ALONE TIME

Disrupters need a significant amount of alone time. They expend a lot of energy thinking, strategising and executing, and prefer to do this by themselves. While Disrupters are happy to plan trips, go to social gatherings and take part in activities on the weekend, these need to fit around their schedule. Given their need for alone time, a Disrupter will often find it easier to be with a similarly independent romantic partner who is equally self-sufficient.

DISRUPTERS ARE LESS EMOTIONAL

Unlike other personality types, Disrupters are less likely to open up and speak about how they feel. Although Disrupters recognise the importance of emotions, they are not often guided by them. Disrupters are naturally more analytical and take time to regularly reassess the relationship's goals and shared vision. For this reason, Disrupters are often suited to personality types who are more emotionally aware and can balance out their rational approach.

Disrupters at Work

DISRUPTERS' DREAM JOB OR WORK ENVIRONMENT

Disrupters are typically drawn to professions that require them to work alone and that involve generating ideas and executing them. They thrive in positions where they set their own deadlines and have fewer social interactions (work gossip is just another distraction for Disrupters!). Work environments and roles where they are micromanaged or are required to attend back-to-back meetings do not suit them, as Disrupters want to spend less time talking and more time doing. They might find it hard to sit still as they are brimming with ideas, so a Disrupter's ideal work environment is one in which they can move around and manage their interactions.

5 Dream Jobs for a Disrupter

| Entrepreneur | Advertising executive | Designer | Product manager | Business analyst |

DISRUPTERS NEED TO EXCEL

Disrupters are naturally gifted learners and absorb information like sponges. They can read multiple books at the same time and will quickly master the most challenging of tasks. At work, Disrupters are able to apply their knowledge quickly and effectively – they are in the envious position of being able to read a few articles and immediately seem like experts. This ability to master subjects and tasks, combined with their natural drive and goal-orientation, makes Disrupters powerhouses in the work environment. They have clear goals in mind, the drive to execute them and the information at their fingertips.

DISRUPTERS ARE INSPIRING LEADERS

Disrupters aren't always people-pleasers, but they often make inspiring leaders. Disrupters strive to create a work environment in which their colleagues and teammates have agency and control over their work, and feel like equals. On a good day, a Disrupter will advocate for trust, respect and giving individuals the freedom to work on their own. While a Disrupter won't provide emotional support, they are happy to dive into a brainstorm or develop a strong shared vision. The ingenuity and creativity of Disrupters coupled with their drive and strong work ethic can make them an example to many.

DISRUPTERS ARE HARD-WORKING

Disrupters are high achievers and not afraid of working late nights. They are action-oriented and passionate about their work, often leading them to put in more than the hours required. They can expect others to work equally hard and may be disappointed to find that not everyone shares the same commitment and drive as they do. As a Disrupter, take care to set realistic expectations of others as well as of yourself, to avoid burnout.

DISRUPTERS ARE LESS ADAPTIVE

As Disrupters do their best work alone, they might struggle to adapt to situations and work scenarios that require them to take on someone else's approach. This can make them less flexible when an authority figure dictates a change in course or strategy. It might even rattle a Disrupter's ego. As a Disrupter, when this happens, try to adopt a beginner's mindset. When our ego tells us that we have figured it out all out, it usually prevents us from seizing a learning opportunity. Remember that other perspectives, no matter how different, can be a rich source of learning.

'You will be
defined not just
by what you
achieve, but by
how you survive.'

*

SHERYL SANDBERG

At Play

DISRUPTERS TAKE SOLO TRIPS

In recreation, as at work, a Disrupter enjoys spending time alone. A solo hiking trip or bike ride is a great way for Disrupters to wind down and take a much-needed break from all that thinking!

DISRUPTERS PRIORITISE WORK OVER PLAY

While Disrupters enjoy social events, they are less likely to be proactive about socialising compared to other personality types, especially when there is work to be done. Disrupters may need more persuading than others to take a break on a weeknight.

DISRUPTERS LEARN NEW SKILLS

Disrupters like mastering a skill. Rather than dabbling in a set of hobbies, Disrupters may have a specific set of skills they want to acquire: for example, learning French, progressing through the grades of scuba diving or gaming.

DISRUPTERS ARE LESS PREOCCUPIED WITH FINANCES

When Disrupters focus on a goal, they become less concerned with financial affairs. While Disrupters may not be spontaneous spenders, they can be late paying bills from time to time as they get side-tracked by pursuing their passion.

DISRUPTERS LIKE TO COMPETE

In line with their driven nature, Disrupters like to set themselves goals and compete to win. For Disrupters who enjoy exercising, running races and difficult endurance events, such as Tough Mudder, are perfect outlets for their competitive nature and can fulfil their need to have a goal to work towards.

A Disrupter's 5 Favourite Apps

Slack * Audible * Evernote * Headspace * LinkedIn

Disrupters and Self-Care

MEDITATE

Given their busy life, it might be challenging for a Disrupter to make time, however, a meditation practice might be a useful way of slowing down. As a Disrupter, set yourself a reminder to meditate. Start with just five minutes per day and gradually increase the time.

DIGITAL DETOX

In our busy lives, we all need a digital detox every so often. Disrupters' drive and goal-orientation can often mean that they rarely get through an evening without checking work emails. As a Disrupter, try to get into the habit of switching off, even if it means putting your phone on airplane mode and leaving it in another room. Do what works best for you.

TAKE A DAY OFF

It can be tempting for a Disrupter to work all hours of the day, especially if they don't do a typical nine-to-five job. However, as a Disrupter, try to protect your Sunday as a day off each week to give yourself a chance to recharge.

REDUCE DECISION-MAKING FATIGUE

Several famous Disrupters, notably Mark Zuckerberg, are known for wearing the same clothes and eating the same meals to free up decision-making powers for the things that matter. As a Disrupter, try wearing the same jeans and t-shirt for a week and see if that reduces your decision-making fatigue and ups your productivity.

REMEMBER YOUR WHY

Given their drive, Disrupters must remember their purpose as this will fuel their motivation and help maintain resilience when times are tough. As a Disrupter, regularly make time to connect with your 'why'.